Perfect Pumpkin Recipes

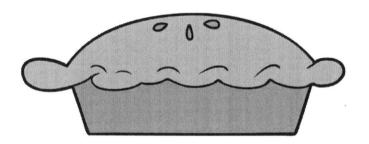

Hannie P. Scott

www.Hanniepscott.com

www.Hanniepscott.com

ISBN: 9781549839399

MY Free Gift to You!

To download your free gift, simply visit:

www.hanniepscott.com/freegift

TABLE OF CONTENTS

For more books by Hannie, please visit:
www.Hanniepscott.com/books

hannie p. scott

Abbreviations

oz = ounce

fl oz = fluid ounce

tsp = teaspoon

tbsp = tablespoon

ml = milliliter

c = cup

pt = pint

qt = quart

gal = gallon

L = liter

conversions

1/2 fl oz = 3 tsp = 1 tbsp = 15 ml

1 fl oz = 2 tbsp = 1/8 c = 30 ml

2 fl oz = 4 tbsp = 1/4 c = 60 ml

4 fl oz = 8 tbsp = 1/2 c = 118 ml

8 fl oz = 16 tbsp = 1 c = 236 ml

16 fl oz = 1 pt = 1/2 qt = 2 c = 473 ml

128 fl oz = 8 pt = 4 qt = 1 gal = 3.78 L

PUMPKIN TREATS

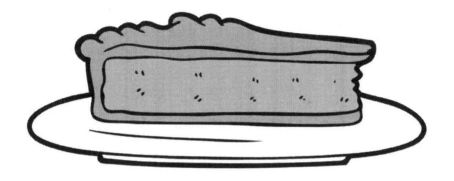

Pumpkin Pie Bars with Pretzel Crust

Servings: 8-10

What you need:

<u>Crust:</u>
- 2 cups pretzels, pulsed into crumbs
- 6 tbsp butter, melted
- 1/3 cup granulated sugar
- 1/2 tsp vanilla
- 1/2 tsp cinnamon
- 1/4 tsp salt

<u>Pumpkin Pie Filling:</u>
- 7 tbsp butter, melted
- 2 1/4 cups sugar
- 8 oz cream cheese, cubed and softened
- 15 oz canned pumpkin
- 3 eggs, at room temperature
- 1 egg yolk, at room temperature
- 2 tsp vanilla extract
- 1 tsp cinnamon
- 1/4 tsp ground ginger
- 1/4 tsp nutmeg
- 1/8 tsp cloves

What to do:

<u>Crust:</u>

1. Line a 9x13-inch baking dish with parchment paper and spray the paper with non-stick cooking spray.
2. Place the pretzels, cinnamon, salt, sugar, and vanilla in a food processor or blender and pulse until combined well.
3. Add the melted butter to the pretzel mixture and stir well.
4. Press the mixture evenly into the prepared pan.

<u>Pumpkin Pie Filling:</u>

1. Preheat your oven to 350 degrees F.
2. Place the sugar in a blender and pulse for about a minute or until it becomes powdery and white.
3. Add the cream cheese and beat for about 2 minutes until light and fluffy.
4. Add the pumpkin and beat for a minute.
5. Add the melted butter and beat for a minute.
6. Add the eggs, vanilla, and spices and blend until well mixed.
7. Pour the mixture over the crust in the prepared pan and spread evenly.
8. Bake for 45-60 minutes or until the center is set.
9. Cool the squares in the pan then cut into pieces and refrigerate before serving.

Pumpkin Bundt Cake

Servings: 8-10

What you need:
- 15 oz can pumpkin
- 4 eggs
- 1 cup vegetable oil
- 2/3 cup water
- 3 cups sugar
- 3 1/2 cups all-purpose flour
- 2 tsp baking soda
- 1 1/2 tsp salt
- 1 tsp cinnamon
- 1 tsp nutmeg
- 1/4 tsp ground ginger
- 1 tsp pumpkin pie spice

What to do:
1. Preheat your oven to 450 degrees F.
2. Spray your bundt cake pan with non-stick spray.
3. In a mixing bowl, mix together the pumpkin, eggs, oil, water, and sugar until thoroughly combined.
4. In a separate bowl, mix together the flour, baking powder, salt, and spices.
5. Add the dry ingredients into the wet ingredients gradually and mix well.
6. Pour the batter into the bundt pan and bake for 45 minutes or until a toothpick inserted into the center comes out clean.
7. Let cool then flip over onto a serving plate before serving.

Pumpkin Crumb Bars

Servings: 10-12

What you need:
- 1 1/4 cups all-purpose flour
- 1 1/4 cups quick oats
- 1/2 tsp salt
- 1/2 tsp baking soda
- 1/2 cup sugar
- 1/2 cup brown sugar
- 3/4 cup butter, melted
- 1 tsp vanilla extract
- 1/4 cup sugar
- 1/4 cup brown sugar
- 1 tsp cinnamon
- 1/2 tsp nutmeg
- 1/4 tsp ginger
- 1 pinch ground cloves
- 1/4 tsp salt
- 1 egg, at room temperature
- 1 egg yolk, at room temperature
- 1/2 tsp vanilla extract
- 1 1/4 cups canned pumpkin
- 1/3 cup evaporated milk
- Whipped cream

What to do:
1. Preheat your oven to 350 degrees F.
2. In a mixing bowl, whisk together the flour, oats, salt, and baking soda until well mixed.

3. Add in the 1/2 cup sugar and 1/2 cup brown sugar and mix well.
4. Add the melted butter and the vanilla and mix well.
5. Press half of the mixture into the bottom of a square baking dish and bake for 15 minutes.
6. In a mixing bowl, whisk together 1/4 cup granulated sugar, 1/4 cup brown sugar, cinnamon, nutmeg, ginger, cloves, and salt.
7. Add in the egg, yolk, and vanilla and stir until mixed well.
8. Mix in the pumpkin and the milk.
9. Pour the mixture over the baked crust in the square dish.
10. Bake for 15 minutes, then remove it from the oven.
11. Sprinkle the rest of the crust crumbs over the top.
12. Return to the oven and bake for another 20-25 minutes or until golden on top.
13. Allow to cool at room temperature then refrigerate for 1 hour before serving.
14. Top with whipped cream before serving.

Pumpkin Spice Pull Apart Bread

Servings: 6

What you need:
- 1 tube Pillsbury Grands Biscuits
- 1 cup sugar
- 1 1/2 tsp pumpkin spice, divided
- 1 cup pumpkin puree
- 1/2 tsp vanilla extract
- 4 oz cream cheese, softened
- 1/2 cup powdered sugar
- 1/2 tsp vanilla extract
- 1/4 tsp pumpkin pie spice
- 1/4 cup milk

What to do:
1. Preheat your oven to 350 degrees F and grease a loaf pan with nonstick spray.
2. Cut the biscuits in half, width-wise, like you're making a sausage biscuit (no sausage in this recipe, I'm just trying to give a mental picture.)
3. Pour the sugar and 1 tsp of pumpkin pie spice into a gallon size zip top bag and shake to combine.
4. Drop the biscuit pieces into the bag, a few at a time, and shake until coated well. Set coated pieces aside.
5. In a medium mixing bowl, combine the pumpkin puree, remaining 1/2 tsp pumpkin pie spice, and vanilla.

6. Use a knife to spread the pumpkin puree onto a biscuit half, and cover it with another biscuit half. Cover the other biscuit half with pumpkin puree too.
7. Do this with all of the biscuits, making a stack of biscuits. When you've covered all the biscuits, place them on their sides in the loaf pan.
8. Bake for 38-40 minutes.
9. While baking, make frosting. Use a mixer to beat the cream cheese until light and fluffy. Add in the powdered sugar, vanilla, and pumpkin pie spice. Gradually add the milk until it's a pourable consistency.
10. Pour the frosting on top of the warm pull apart bread after you've taken it from the oven.

Pumpkin Butter

Servings: 10-12

What you need:
- 2 12-oz cans of pumpkin
- 1/2 cup apple cider
- 2/3 cup sugar
- 1/4 cup brown sugar
- 1 tbsp pumpkin pie spice
- 1 tsp vanilla
- 1/2 tsp kosher salt

What to do:
1. Pour all the ingredients into your slow cooker and stir until smooth.
2. Cover and cook for 3 hours on high, stirring every hour.
3. Store in mason jars in your refrigerator.

Pumpkin Pie Spice

Servings: 9

What you need:
- 2 tbsp cinnamon
- 2 tsp nutmeg
- 2 tsp ground ginger
- 1 tsp allspice
- 1 tsp cloves

What to do:
1. Mix all of the ingredients together and store in an airtight container.

Pumpkin Rice Krispie Treats With Frosting

Servings: 12-14

What you need:

- 2 tbsp butter
- 10 oz mini marshmallows
- 6 cups Rice Krispies
- 1 tbsp pumpkin pie spice
- 1 cup butterscotch chips
- 1 cup powdered sugar
- 2 tbsp brown sugar
- 1 tsp cinnamon
- 1 tsp vanilla extract
- 2.5 tbsp milk

What to do:

1. Spray a 9x13-inch pan with non-stick cooking spray.
2. Add the butter to a large saucepan over low heat and let it melt.
3. Add the marshmallows and stir until they are melted.
4. Add the Rice Krispies and the pumpkin pie spice and stir until well coated with the marshmallows.
5. Add the butterscotch chips and stir to combine.
6. Pour the mixture into the prepared pan and press it down evenly.
7. Let the Rice Krispies cool to room temperature.

8. To make the frosting, combine the powdered sugar, brown sugar, cinnamon, vanilla extract, and milk. Drizzle the mixture over the bars.
9. Cut into squares before serving.

Pumpkin Rice Krispie Treats

Servings: 8-10

What you need:
- 4 tbsp butter
- 4 cups marshmallows
- 2 tbsp canned pumpkin
- 1/2 tsp pumpkin pie spice
- 6 cups Rice Krispies cereal

What to do:
1. Melt the butter in a large saucepan over medium-low heat.
2. Stir in the marshmallows and stir until they are melted.
3. Add in the pumpkin and pumpkin pie spice and stir well.
4. Pour in the Rice Krispies cereal and stir well.
5. Pour the mixture into a greased 9x13 inch baking pan and flatten out the mixture.
6. When the treats are cooled, cut them and serve!

Pumpkin Cream Cheese Brownies

Servings: 10-12

What you need:

- 1 box brownie mix plus ingredients the instructions call for
- 1 large egg
- 4 oz cream cheese, softened
- 1/2 cup canned pumpkin
- 1/4 cup sugar
- 2 tsp pumpkin pie spice
- 3 tbsp all-purpose flour

What to do:

1. Preheat your oven to 350 degrees F and line an 8-inch square baking pan with parchment paper, leaving some hanging over the sides for easy lifting.
2. Prepare the brownie batter according to box instructions.
3. Pour half of the brownie batter into the prepared pan.
4. Bake for 15 minutes. It won't be all the way done, that's ok.
5. In a medium mixing bowl, add the egg, cream cheese, pumpkin, sugar, and pumpkin pie spice. Mix well.
6. Add the flour to the pumpkin mixture and mix until combined.
7. Evenly spread this mixture over the cooked brownies in the pan.
8. Evenly spread the other half of the brownie batter on top of the pumpkin mixture.

9. Bake for 23-25 minutes or until a toothpick inserted into the middle comes out without brownie batter on it. It's okay if there is pumpkin mixture on the toothpick.
10. Let cool and cut into squares before serving.

Pumpkin Cream Cheese Truffles

Servings: 12

What you need:
- 12 oz of white chocolate chips
- 1 cup canned pumpkin
- 1 cup finely crushed graham crackers
- 4 oz cream cheese, softened

What to do:
1. Place 3 oz of the chocolate chips in a microwave safe bowl and heat 20 seconds at a time until melted and smooth. Stir after every 20 second increment.
2. Stir in the cream cheese, pumpkin, and pumpkin pie spice and mix together well.
3. Stir in the crushed graham crackers, reserve a couple tbsps.
4. Place the bowl in the freezer for 45 minutes or until firm.
5. Line a baking sheet with parchment paper.
6. Form 1" balls from the mixture and place the balls on the prepared baking sheet.
7. Melt the rest of the chocolate chip using the same method as step 1.
8. Dip each ball into the melted chocolate and place back onto the baking sheet.
9. Sprinkle the remaining crushed graham crackers over the truffles.
10. Place in the freezer for 10 minutes before serving.

Pumpkin Pie Dip

Servings: 6-8

What you need:

- 8 oz cream cheese spread, at room temperature
- 1 cup canned pumpkin
- 1 cup powdered sugar
- 1 1/2 tsp pumpkin pie spice
- 1 tsp cinnamon
- 1/2 tsp vanilla
- 1/2 container whipped cream

What to do:

1. With an electric mixer in a large bowl, cream together all of the ingredients until blended well and smooth.
2. Cover and refrigerate until ready to serve.
3. Serve with graham crackers or vanilla wafers.

Pumpkin Pie Spice Popcorn

Servings: 20

What you need:

- 10 cups popped popcorn
- 1/2 cup butter
- 1 cup brown sugar
- 1/4 cup corn syrup
- 1 1/2 tsp cinnamon
- 3/4 tsp ground nutmeg
- 3/4 tsp ground ginger
- 1/4 tsp ground cloves
- 1/2 tsp salt
- 1 tsp vanilla extract
- 1/4 tsp baking soda
- 5 oz white chocolate chips

What to do:

1. Preheat your oven to 250 degrees F.
2. Place your popcorn in a very large bowl and remove any unpopped kernels.
3. In a medium saucepan over medium heat, melt the butter.
4. Stir the brown sugar, corn syrup, cinnamon, nutmeg, ginger, cloves, and salt into the melted butter in the saucepan and bring it to a boil. Let it boil for 3-5 minutes or until it looks caramel-like.
5. Remove it from the heat and stir in the vanilla and baking soda and stir well.

6. Pour half the caramel sauce over the popcorn and toss to coat evenly.
7. Spread the popcorn onto a large baking sheet (or two) in an even layer and bake for 1 hour. Stir every 15 minutes.
8. When the popcorn is done, place the chocolate chips in a microwave safe bowl and microwave 15 seconds at a time until they are melted.
9. Drizzle the white chocolate over the popcorn and let cool.

No-Bake Pumpkin Cheesecake

Servings: 8-10

What you need:

- 1 8-oz package of cream cheese, softened
- 1 cup canned pumpkin
- 2 1/2 cups whipped cream
- 1/2 cup sugar
- 1/2 tsp pumpkin pie spice
- 1 premade graham cracker crust

What to do:

1. In a medium bowl, cream together the softened cream cheese and sugar with a mixer.
2. Add in the pumpkin puree and pumpkin pie spice until well mixed.
3. Fold in the whipped cream.
4. Pour the mixture into the graham cracker crust and refrigerate for 2-4 hours before serving.

Brown Sugar Pumpkin Pie

Servings: 8-10

What you need:
- 1 9-inch deep dish frozen pie shell
- 2 tbsp butter, melted
- 1 cup brown sugar, packed
- 1 15-oz can of pumpkin
- 3 eggs
- 1 cup heavy cream
- 1/2 cup sour cream
- 1 tbsp pumpkin pie spice
- 2 tsp vanilla extract

What to do:
1. Prepare the pie shell according to package directions.
2. Preheat your oven to 425 degrees F.
3. In a mixing bowl, mix the butter, brown sugar, and pumpkin until well mixed.
4. Add the eggs, heavy cream, sour cream, pumpkin pie spice, and vanilla to the mixing bowl and mix until thoroughly combined.
5. Pour the batter into the pie shell, all the way to the top, but don't overfill.
6. Place the pie in the oven and bake for 15 minutes at 425 degrees F then reduce the heat to 350 degrees F and bake for another 45-50 minutes. The pie should still jiggle in the center a little bit.
7. Remove the pie from the oven and allow it to cool for 2-3 hours before serving.

Pumpkin Pie Muddy Buddies

Servings: 16

What you need:
- 8 cups Chex cereal
- 12 oz white chocolate chips
- 1/2 cup canned pumpkin
- 2 cups powdered sugar
- 3 tsp pumpkin pie spice
- 1 cup fall colored M&Ms

What to do:
1. Place the white chocolate chips in a microwave safe bowl and heat 20 seconds at a time until melted and smooth. Stir after every 20 second increment.
2. Add the pumpkin to the white chocolate and stir well.
3. Add the Chex to a very large mixing bowl and pour the chocolate/pumpkin mixture over the Chex. Toss to coat well.
4. Place the powdered sugar and the pumpkin pie spice to a gallon sized zip lock bag and shake or stir together.
5. Add the Chex mixture to the powdered sugar in the zip lock bag and shake well to coat.
6. Pour the mixture into a large bowl and toss in the M&Ms before serving.

PUMPKIN PIE APPLE CRISP

Servings: 8-10

What you need:
- 1 cup pumpkin pie filling
- 1/4 cup evaporated milk
- 1 egg
- 1 tsp pumpkin pie spice
- 4 apples, peeled and chopped
- 1/2 cup brown sugar
- 1/4 cup white sugar
- 1 tbsp cinnamon
- 1/4 cup brown sugar
- 1/2 cup oats
- 1/4 cup melted butter

What to do:
1. Preheat your oven to 375 degrees and spray a square baking dish with non-stick spray.
2. Mix together the pumpkin pie filling, evaporated milk, egg, and pumpkin pie spice in a mixing bowl.
3. Place the mixture into the bottom of the square baking pan and bake for 10 minutes then remove from the oven.
4. Mix the chopped apples with the brown sugar, white sugar, and cinnamon.
5. Pour the apples on top of the pumpkin layer in the baking dish.
6. Mix together the brown sugar, oats, and melted butter and sprinkle it over the apples.
7. Bake for 40-45 minutes.

Pumpkin Pie Fudge

Servings: 10-12

What you need:
- 3 cups sugar
- 1/2 can evaporated milk
- 1/3 cup corn syrup
- 1 stick butter
- 1/2 cup canned pumpkin
- 1 tsp pumpkin pie spice

What to do:
1. Mix the sugar, evaporated milk, corn syrup, pumpkin, and pumpkin spice in a large saucepan over medium heat and bring to a low boil. Stir occasionally.
2. Use a candy thermometer and remove the mixture from the heat when it reaches 235-245 degrees F.
3. Grease the inside of a baking dish with butter. Add the rest of the butter to the mixture and stir until the butter is melted.
4. Pour the mixture into the buttered baking dish.
5. Refrigerate for 2-3 hours before cutting and serving.

Pumpkin Pie Pudding

Servings: 8

What you need:
- 1 large box of instant vanilla pudding
- 2 cups milk
- 1 can of pumpkin
- 6 oz cool whip
- 2 tsp pumpkin pie spice
- Ginger snaps or vanilla wafers

What to do:
1. Prepare the vanilla pudding according to package directions then refrigerate it for 10 minutes.
2. Stir in the pumpkin, cool whip, and pumpkin pie spice and mix well.
3. Refrigerate for at least 30 minutes.
4. Serve with ginger snaps or vanilla wafers.

Pumpkin Pie Truffles

Servings: 12

What you need:
- 1 cup canned pumpkin
- 1 cup powdered sugar
- 1 cup flour
- 1 tbsp coconut oil
- 2 tsp cinnamon
- 2 tsp pumpkin pie spice
- 1 tsp vanilla extract
- 1 1/2 cup chocolate chips

What to do:
1. In a mixing bowl, mix together the pumpkin, powdered sugar, flour, coconut oil, pumpkin pie spice, and vanilla.
2. Place the bowl in your freezer for 45 minutes.
3. Place parchment paper on a baking pan.
4. Roll the mixture into 1 inch balls and place them on the prepared baking pan.
5. Place the chocolate chips in a microwave safe bowl and heat 20 seconds at a time until melted and smooth. Stir after every 20 second increment.
6. Dip the pumpkin balls into the chocolate and coat well. Place them back on the baking pan.
7. Refrigerate for an hour before serving.

PumPkin Dessert Lasagna

Servings: 10

What you need:

Crust:
- 1 cup flour
- 1/2 cup butter, softened
- 1/2 cup chopped pecans, toasted

Cheesecake layer:
- 8 oz cream cheese, softened
- 1 cup powdered sugar
- 1 cup whipped cream

Pumpkin layer:
- 2 1/2 cups milk
- 3 small packages of instant pudding mix
- 15 oz canned pumpkin
- 1 tsp cinnamon
- Topping:
- 2 cups whipped cream
- 1/2 cup chopped pecans, toasted

What to do:

1. Preheat your oven to 350 degrees F and spray a square baking dish with non-stick spray.
2. Mix the ingredients for the crust in a mixing bowl and press into the prepared square baking dish.
3. Bake for 15 minutes then remove from the oven.
4. Mix the cream cheese and powdered sugar in a mixing bowl until its light and fluffy.

5. Add the 1 cup of whipped cream into the mixture and mix well.
6. Spread the cream cheese mixture over the crust and place in the refrigerator.
7. In another bowl, mix together the pudding mix, pumpkin, and cinnamon until smooth. Spread this mixture over the cream cheese layer.
8. Spread the remaining whipped cream over the pumpkin layer and sprinkle with pecans.
9. Refrigerate for 2-4 hours before serving.

Pumpkin Angel Food Cake

Servings: 12

What you need:
- 1 box angel food cake mix
- 15 oz can of pumpkin
- 1 tsp pumpkin pie spice
- 8 tbsp butter
- 8 oz of cream cheese, softened
- 1/2 tsp vanilla extract
- 2 1/2 cups powdered sugar
- 1 tsp cinnamon

What to do:
1. Preheat your oven to 350 degrees F and spray a 9x13 inch baking dish with non-stick spray.
2. In a large bowl, mix together the angel food cake mix and the pumpkin pie space.
3. Stir in the pumpkin until well combined.
4. Pour the mixture into the prepared pan and bake for 25-30 minutes.
5. Remove from the oven and let the cake cool completely.
6. With a mixer, cream together the butter and cream cheese until light and fluffy.
7. Add in the vanilla and mix.
8. Slowly mix in the powdered sugar and cinnamon.
9. Mix until everything is mixed together and light and fluffy.
10. Frost the cake with this mixture and cut into bars before serving.

Pumpkin Pecan Bread Pudding

Servings: 8

What you need:
- 8 cups cubed bread
- 1/2 cup chopped toasted pecans
- 1/2 cup butterscotch chips
- 4 eggs
- 1 cup canned pumpkin
- 1 cup half-and-half
- 1/2 cup packed brown sugar
- 1/2 cup butter, melted
- 1 tsp vanilla
- 1/2 tsp cinnamon
- 1/2 tsp nutmeg
- 1/4 tsp ground ginger
- 1/8 tsp ground cloves

What to do:
1. Put the cubed bread into your crock pot.
2. Add in the butterscotch chips and the toasted pecans.
3. In a separate bowl, whisk together the eggs, pumpkin, half-n-half, brown sugar, butter, vanilla, cinnamon, nutmeg, ginger, and cloves.
4. Pour this mixture over the cubed bread in the crock pot and gently stir to make sure everything is coated.
5. Cook on low for 3-4 hours or until set.

Pumpkin Bread

Servings: 8-10

What you need:
- 1 cup sugar
- 1/2 cup oil
- 2 eggs
- 1 cup canned pumpkin
- 1 1/2 cup sifted all-purpose flour
- 1/4 tsp salt
- 1/4 tsp baking powder
- 1/2 tsp baking soda
- 1/2 tsp ground cloves
- 1/2 tsp cinnamon
- 1/2 tsp ground nutmeg
- 1/2 cup brown sugar
- 1/3 cup flour
- 1/4 cup butter

What to do:
1. Preheat your oven to 350 degrees F.
2. Grease and flour a loaf pan
3. In a large bowl, beat the sugar and oil until they are mixed well.
4. Add in the eggs, one at a time, and beating well until light and fluffy.
5. Mix in the pumpkin.
6. Add in the flour, salt, baking powder, baking soda, cloves, cinnamon, and nutmeg. Mix well.
7. Pour this mixture into the loaf pan.

8. In another bowl, mix together the brown sugar, flour, and butter.
9. Spread this mixture over the batter in the loaf pan.
10. Bake for an hour or until a toothpick inserted comes out clean.

Pumpkin Pie

Servings: 8

What you need:
- 1 graham cracker crust
- 1 15-oz can pumpkin pie filling
- 1 8-oz container whipped cream
- 1 tsp cinnamon
- 8-oz cream cheese

What to do:
1. In a medium bowl, whip the cream cheese until it has fluffed up some.
2. Slowly add the pumpkin pie filling and cinnamon to the cream cheese and mix on low until they are mixed together well.
3. Mix in the whipped cream.
4. Pour the mixture into the pie crust.
5. Refrigerate for at least 2 hours before serving.

Pumpkin Trifle

Servings: 10-12

What you need:
- 1 spice cake box mix
- 1 1/4 cups water
- 1 egg
- 4 cups milk
- 4 oz package instant butterscotch pudding mix
- 1 15-oz pumpkin pie mix
- 12-oz container whipped topping

What to do:
1. For the cake, mix the ingredients and bake in an 8x8 baking pan for 35 minutes at 350 degrees F. Let the cake cool then crumble it.
2. For the pudding, mix the milk with the pudding mix and stir out any lumps. When the pudding is set, add the pumpkin pie mix.
3. Layer the trifle in the following order: 1/4 of the cake crumbles, half of the pudding mixture, 1/4 of the cake crumbles, half of the whipped topping. Repeat the layers.
4. Garnish the trifle with whipped topping and cake crumbs.

PumPKin Bars

Servings: 8-10

What you need:
- 2 cups flour
- 2 tsp baking powder
- 2 tsp cinnamon
- 1/2 tsp nutmeg
- 1 tsp salt
- 1 tsp baking soda
- 4 eggs
- 1 2/3 cup sugar
- 1 cup oil
- 1 15-oz can pumpkin
- 8 oz cream cheese, softened
- 1/3 cup butter
- 3 cups powdered sugar
- 1 cup whipped cream
- 1 tbsp milk

What to do:
1. Preheat your oven to 350 degrees F and grease a 15x10 baking pan.
2. In a small bowl, sift together the flour, baking powder, cinnamon, nutmeg, salt, and baking soda.
3. In a large mixing bowl, combine the eggs, sugar, oil, and pumpkin until mixed well.
4. Gradually mix in the dry ingredients and mix well.

5. Spread the batter into the baking dish and bake for 25-30 minutes or until a toothpick inserted into the center comes out clean.
6. While the bars are in the oven, place the cream cheese and butter in a mixing bowl and cream together.
7. Add in the powdered sugar, whipped cream, vanilla extract, and milk. Mix until fluffy.
8. Place the frosting in the refrigerator.
9. When the bars are finished cooking, let them cool completely then frost them generously.

Pumpkin Brownies

Servings: 8-10

What you need:

- 1 boxed brownie mix
- 1 15-oz can pumpkin

What to do:

1. Preheat your oven to 350 degrees F and spray a 9x13-inch pan with nonstick spray.
2. Mix together the brownie mix and pumpkin in a large bowl.
3. Pour the batter into the baking pan and bake for 25-30 minutes or until a toothpick inserted into the center comes out clean.

Pumpkin Fudge

Servings: 18-20

What you need:
- 3 cups sugar
- 3/4 cup butter, melted
- 2/3 cup evaporated milk
- 1 cup canned pumpkin
- 2 tbsp corn syrup
- 2 1/2 tsp pumpkin pie spice
- 9 oz white chocolate chips
- 7 oz marshmallow fluff
- 1 tsp vanilla extract

What to do:
1. Line a 9x13 inch pan with parchment paper, grease it, and set it aside.
2. In a large saucepan over medium-high heat, stir together the sugar, butter, evaporated milk, canned pumpkin, corn syrup, and pumpkin pie spice. Stir constantly until the mixture comes to a boil. Stir until a thermometer reads 235 degrees F.
3. Remove the pan from the heat and stir in the white chocolate chips, marshmallow fluff, and vanilla until it's all mixed together.
4. Pour the mixture into the prepared pan and refrigerate until completely cooled.
5. Cut into squares and serve.

Pumpkin Dip

Servings: 8-10

What you need:
- 8 oz cream cheese, softened
- 1 cup brown sugar
- 1 tsp ground ginger
- 1/2 tsp ground nutmeg
- 2 tsp cinnamon
- 1 15-oz can pumpkin puree

What to do:
1. With a hand mixer, mix the cream cheese in a mixing bowl until it is smooth.
2. Add the brown sugar, ginger, nutmeg, and cinnamon and blend well.
3. Add in the pumpkin puree and mix well.
4. Refrigerate until chilled then serve with cookies or fruit.

No-Bake Mini Pumpkin Cheesecakes

Servings: 8-10

What you need:
- 1 sleeve of graham crackers
- 1/2 stick of butter, melted
- 1 tbsp sugar
- 2 tbsp brown sugar
- 8-oz cream cheese, softened
- 1 15-oz can pumpkin puree
- 3 tsp pumpkin pie spice
- 1 1-oz package cheesecake instant pudding mix
- 1 14-oz can sweetened condensed milk
- 1 8-oz container whipped cream

What to do:
1. In a food processor, pulse the graham crackers until they are a fine crumb.
2. Add in the melted butter, sugar, and brown sugar and pulse until combined well.
3. Spoon the crumbs into individual 8-10 oz cups.
4. Place the cups in the refrigerator to set.
5. In a mixing bowl, whip the cream cheese with a mixer until creamy.
6. Add in the pumpkin and mix until combined well.
7. Add in the sweetened condensed milk and mix until combined well.
8. Gently mix in the whipped cream.

9. Top the graham cracker crusts in each cup with the cheesecake mixture and refrigerate for an hour or two until ready to serve.

PUMPKIN ROLLS

Servings: 16

What you need:

- 2 packages canned crescent rolls
- 4 oz cream cheese, softened
- 1/2 cup powdered sugar
- 1/4 cup pumpkin
- 1/4 tsp ground cinnamon
- 1/4 tsp allspice
- 2 tbsp cream cheese, softened
- 1 cup powdered sugar
- 1 tbsp milk
- 1 tbsp sweetened condensed milk
- 1 tbsp butter, melted
- 1/4 cup cinnamon/sugar mixture

What to do:

1. Preheat your oven to 375 degrees F.
2. In a large mixing bowl, beat together the cream cheese, 1/2 cup powdered sugar, pumpkin, cinnamon, and allspice until well mixed.
3. Line a large baking pan with parchment paper and unroll each crescent roll onto the pan.
4. Spoon a spoonful of pumpkin mixture onto each crescent roll.
5. Roll up each crescent roll.
6. Mix together the 1 tbsp of melted butter and cinnamon/sugar mixture.
7. Brush each rolled up crescent roll with the butter/cinnamon/sugar mixture.

8. Bake for 11-13 minutes or until golden brown then let them cool.
9. While the crescents are baking and cooling, whisk together the 2 tbsp of softened cream cheese, 1 cup powdered sugar and milk and drizzle over the crescent rolls when they are slightly cooled.

PUMPKIN BREAKFASTS

Pumpkin Pie French Toast

Servings: 4

What you need:
- 3 large eggs
- 1/2 cup milk
- 3/4 cup pumpkin puree
- 1 tsp pumpkin pie spice
- 8 slices of bread

What to do:
1. Whisk together the eggs, pumpkin puree, pumpkin pie spice, and milk in a shallow bowl.
2. Heat a skillet over medium heat and spray with nonstick spray.
3. Dredge each slice of bread in the egg mixture on both sides.
4. Place however many slices of soaked bread in the skillet as will fit and cook for 2-3 minutes on each side.
5. Cook all of the slices until they are all cooked.
6. Serve with your topping of choice.

Pumpkin Chocolate Chip Muffins

Servings: 24

What you need:
- 4 eggs
- 2 cups sugar
- 1 15-oz can of pumpkin
- 1 1/2 cups canola oil
- 2 cups all-purpose flour
- 2 tsp baking soda
- 1 tsp baking powder
- 1 tbsp pumpkin pie spice
- 1 tsp salt
- 2 cups chocolate chips

What to do:
1. Preheat your oven to 400 degrees F and place liners in a muffin pan.
2. In a large bowl, mix together the eggs, sugar, pumpkin and oil until smooth.
3. In another bowl, mix together the flour, baking soda, baking powder, pumpkin pie spice, and salt.
4. Mix the flour mixture into the pumpkin mixture.
5. Fold in the chocolate chips.
6. Fill the muffin liners 3/4 way full with the batter.
7. Bake for 15-17 minutes or until a toothpick inserted into the center of a muffin comes out clean.
8. Cool for 10 minutes before serving.

Pumpkin Waffles

Servings: 4-6

What you need:
- 2 large eggs
- 1 1/2 cups buttermilk
- 1 stick butter, melted
- 1 tsp vanilla extract
- 1/2 cup pumpkin puree
- 1 3/4 cups all-purpose flour
- 2 tsp pumpkin pie spice
- 3 tbsp sugar
- 2 tsp baking powder
- 1 tsp baking soda
- 1 tsp salt

What to do:
1. Preheat your waffle maker.
2. In a mixing bowl, mix together the eggs, buttermilk, butter, vanilla, and pumpkin puree until well mixed.
3. In a separate bowl, combine the flour, pumpkin pie spice, sugar, baking powder, baking soda, and salt.
4. Slowly add the dry ingredients to the wet ingredients and mix well.
5. Spray your waffle maker with non-stick spray and scoop batter onto the maker 1 cup at a time.
6. Cook until the waffle is done then repeat until the batter is gone.
7. Serve with syrup, whipped cream, pecans, or your choice of topping.

Pumpkin Pie Crescents

Servings: 16

What you need:
- 2 tubes crescent rolls
- 8 oz cream cheese, softened
- 1 cup canned pumpkin pie filling
- 4 tbsp sugar
- 1 tbsp pumpkin pie spice

What to do:
1. Preheat your oven to 350 degrees F.
2. Unroll each crescent roll and cut them each in half lengthwise.
3. Beat together the cream cheese and pumpkin pie filling in a mixing bowl until it is fluffy.
4. Spread about 2 tsp of the filling on each crescent roll half and roll them up starting with the wide end.
5. Mix together the 4 tbsp of sugar and the 1 tbsp of pumpkin pie spice in a small bowl.
6. Roll each crescent in the sugar and spice mix.
7. Place each roll on a greased baking sheet and bake for 13-15 minutes or until golden brown.

Pumpkin Pie Oatmeal

Servings: 2

What you need:
- 2 cups quick oats
- 1 1/4 cups almond milk
- 3/4 cup canned pumpkin
- 1 tbsp brown sugar
- 2 tsp pumpkin pie spice
- Pinch of salt
- 1/4 cup butterscotch chips
- 1/4 cup white chocolate chips
- 1/4 cup chopped pecans

What to do:
1. In a microwave safe bowl, stir together the oats, almond milk, pumpkin, brown sugar, pumpkin pie spice, and salt.
2. Microwave for 2 minutes.
3. Top with pecans, butterscotch chips, and white chocolate chips and serve.

PUMPKIN DISHES

Pumpkin Mac and Cheese

Servings: 4

What you need:
- 16-oz macaroni pasta
- 2 cups half and half
- 2 tbsp flour
- 2 tbsp butter
- 2 cups shredded sharp cheddar cheese
- 1 15-oz can of pumpkin puree
- Salt and pepper, to taste
- 1/2 cup panko crumbs

What to do:
1. In a large pot, cook the macaroni according to package directions, to al dente.
2. Meanwhile, in a large saucepan, add the half and half, flour, and butter. Cook and stir over medium heat until the mixture is slightly thickened.
3. Add the cheese and pumpkin to the half and half mixture and stir until the cheese is melted.
4. Add the cooked macaroni to the cheese mixture and stir to coat. Add salt and pepper.
5. Pour into a casserole dish and top with panko. Bake at 400 degrees F for 20 minutes.

Pumpkin Beef Stew

Servings: 8

What you need:
- 3 lbs beef stew meat
- 1/2 cup all-purpose flour
- 3 tbsp butter
- 1 small onion, chopped
- 1 clove garlic, minced
- 1 quart beef broth
- 2 cups pumpkin puree
- 1 tbsp Worcestershire sauce
- 1 tbsp sea salt
- 1 tsp ground black pepper
- 3 lbs potatoes, peeled and diced
- 1 lb carrots, peeled and sliced
- 4 sprigs of thyme

What to do:
1. Dredge the beef stew meat in flour until coated.
2. In a large saucepan, melt the butter over medium-high heat and brown the beef. Work in batches if needed.
3. Remove beef from pan and set aside.
4. Once all beef is browned, add the onion and garlic to the pan and sauté for 3 minutes.
5. Return the browned beef to the pan and add the beef broth, pumpkin puree, Worcestershire, salt, and pepper. Stir and bring to a boil.
6. Reduce heat to medium-low and simmer for 3 hours, stirring occasionally.

7. Add the potatoes, carrots, and thyme. Cook for another hour. Make sure potatoes are cooked through before serving.

Pumpkin Hummus

Makes 2.5 cups

What you need:
- 1 15-oz can of chick peas, rinsed and drained
- 1 cup canned pumpkin puree
- 1/4 cup water
- 10 sage leaves, roughly chopped
- 1 1/2 tbsp olive oil
- 1 1/2 tsp salt
- 2 sage leaves, chopped small, for garnish

What to do:
1. Place all of the ingredients, except the sage leaves used for garnish, in a food processor and process until smooth, scraping down the sides as needed.
2. Transfer the hummus to a serving bowl and garnish with chopped sage.
3. Cover and refrigerate for an hour or more then serve with pita bread or naan.

PUMPKIN DRINKS

Harry Potter Pumpkin Juice

Makes 48 oz

SPECIAL NOTE: Just in case you did not know, I absolutely love Harry Potter. I've read all the books multiple times, I've watched all the movies more times than I can remember, and I've been to Harry Potter World ☺

What you need:
- 1 can of frozen apple juice concentrate, plus 2 cans water
- 1/2 cup of canned pumpkin
- 1/4 cup apricot preserves
- 1/2 tsp vanilla extract
- 1/4 tsp pumpkin pie spice

What to do:
1. Blend all of the ingredients.
2. Pour into glasses then serve.

Warm Pumpkin Drink

Servings: 4-6

What you need:
- 4 cups whipping cream
- 2 cups whole milk
- 3/4 cup sugar
- 15 oz canned pumpkin
- 1/4 tsp ground cinnamon
- 1/8 tsp ground ginger
- 1/8 tsp ground nutmeg
- 1/16 tsp allspice
- 1/16 tsp ground cloves
- 1 tsp vanilla extract
- Whipped cream

What to do:
1. Stir together the cream, milk, and sugar in a saucepan over medium heat until the sugar is dissolved.
2. Whisk in the pumpkin, spices, and vanilla until well mixed.
3. Simmer on low for 15-20 minutes.
4. Serve topped with whipped cream.

Easy Pumpkin Spice Latte

Servings: 2

What you need:
- 1/2 cup pumpkin puree
- 1 cup French vanilla liquid coffee creamer
- 2 tsp pumpkin pie spice
- 1 1/2 cups hot strong coffee
- Whipped cream
- Cinnamon

What to do:
1. In a medium saucepan over medium heat, whisk together the pumpkin puree, coffee creamer, and pumpkin pie spice until smooth.
2. Reduce the heat to low and simmer for 5 minutes.
3. Pour in the coffee.
4. Pour into coffee mugs and top with whipped cream and cinnamon.
5. Serve immediately.

Pumpkin Spice Latte

Servings: 12 (syrup), 1 (latte)

What you need:

For the syrup:
- 1 1/2 cup water
- 1 1/2 cup sugar
- 1/3 cup pumpkin puree
- 1 1/2 tsp cinnamon
- 1 tsp nutmeg
- 1/2 tsp cloves
- 1/2 tsp ginger

For the latte:
- 8 oz milk
- 4 oz strong coffee
- 2 tbsp pumpkin spice syrup
- Whipped cream
- Pumpkin pie spice

What to do:

Syrup:
1. In a pan over medium heat, stir together the water and sugar and let it simmer until the sugar is dissolved.
2. Add the cinnamon, nutmeg, cloves, and ginger and stir well.
3. Add the pumpkin, mix well, and let it simmer for 10 minutes. Stir every minute or so.
4. Remove the mixture from the heat and strain it.

5. Let the syrup cool then pour it into an airtight container and refrigerate.

<u>Latte</u>:
1. Heat the milk in the microwave for 1 minute.
2. Whisk the milk vigorously to make it frothy.
3. Put 2 tbsp of syrup into the bottom of a coffee cup.
4. Pour the strong coffee into the coffee cup.
5. Pour the frothy milk into the coffee cup.
6. Top with whipped cream and sprinkle on some pumpkin pie spice.

Pumpkin Spice Frappuccino

Servings: 2

What you need:
- 1 1/2 cups strong coffee, frozen then partially defrosted
- 2 tbsp canned pumpkin
- 1/2 tsp vanilla extract
- 1/4 tsp pumpkin spice
- 1 tsp sugar
- 1/2 cup coconut milk
- Whipped cream
- Cinnamon

What to do:
1. In a blender, add the coffee, pumpkin, vanilla, pumpkin spice, sugar, and coconut milk. Blend until smooth and creamy.
2. Pour the drink into two glasses and top with whipped cream and a sprinkle of cinnamon.

Pumpkin Pie White Hot Chocolate

Servings: 4

What you need:
- 3 cups milk
- 1 cup canned pumpkin
- 1/2 tsp cinnamon
- 1/4 tsp ginger
- 1/8 tsp cloves
- 1/8 tsp nutmeg
- 1 tsp vanilla
- 4 oz white chocolate chips
- A pinch of salt
- Whipped cream
- Cinnamon

What to do:
1. In a medium saucepan over medium heat, stir together the milk, pumpkin, and spices. Let it simmer.
2. Remove the saucepan from the heat and stir in the white chocolate chips and stir until they are melted.
3. Pour into mugs and top with whipped cream and a sprinkle of cinnamon.

Pumpkin Spice White Hot Chocolate

Servings: 2

What you need:
- 1 cup heavy cream
- 2 cups milk
- 1 tbsp canned pumpkin
- 1 cup white chocolate chips
- 1/2 tsp vanilla extract
- 1/2 tsp pumpkin spice
- Whipped cream

What to do:
1. In a medium sauce pan over medium heat, stir together the heavy cream, milk, and pumpkin. Stir until its steaming but don't let it boil.
2. Pour the hot mixture into a medium sized bowl and add the white chocolate chips. Stir until the chips are melted.
3. Add the vanilla extract and the pumpkin spice.
4. Pour into glasses and top with whipped cream.

Salted Caramel Pumpkin Spice Latte

Servings: 2

What you need:
- 2 cups milk
- 4 tbsp canned pumpkin
- 3 tbsp caramel sauce, divided
- 1 tbsp vanilla extract
- 1/2 tsp pumpkin pie spice
- 1 cup strong coffee
- 1/2 cup whipped cream
- 1/4 tsp sea salt

What to do:
1. In a small saucepan, mix together the milk, pumpkin, 2 tbsp of the caramel, vanilla extract, and pumpkin pie spice. Whisk together and simmer for 3-5 minutes over medium-low heat. Don't let it boil.
2. Remove from heat and pour the mixture into a blender. Pulse until frothy, about 1 minute.
3. Pour the mixture into 2 mugs.
4. Pour 1/2 cup coffee in each mug and gently stir.
5. Top each drink with whipped cream, the remaining caramel, and sea salt.

Pumpkin Spice Chai Latte

Servings: 1

What you need:
- 1 tbsp canned pumpkin
- 1 tsp brown sugar
- 1 tsp vanilla extract
- 1 tsp pumpkin spice
- 1/4 tsp salt
- 1 cup milk
- 1 chai tea bag
- Whipped cream
- Cinnamon

What to do:
1. In a small bowl, mix together the canned pumpkin, brown sugar, vanilla extract, pumpkin spice and salt.
2. Place the chai tea bag in a large coffee mug and pour 4 oz of boiling water over the bag.
3. In a medium saucepan over medium heat, stir together the pumpkin mixture from step 1 and the milk. Stir until it thickens but don't let it boil.
4. Pour the hot milk into the tea.
5. Top with whipped cream and a dash of cinnamon.

Crock Pot Pumpkin Spice Latte

Servings: 6-8

What you need:
- 3 cups milk
- 3 cups strongly brewed coffee
- 1/2 cup canned pumpkin
- 1/3 cup vanilla coffee creamer
- 1 tbsp vanilla extract
- 1/3 cup sugar
- 2 tsp cinnamon

What to do:
1. Pour the coffee and the milk into your crock pot.
2. In a small bowl, whisk together the pumpkin, vanilla coffee creamer, vanilla extract, sugar, and cinnamon. Pour it into the crock pot.
3. Whisk everything together well in the crock pot.
4. Cook on high for 2 hours.

Pumpkin Spice Hot Chocolate

Servings: 2

What you need:
- 2 1/2 cups milk
- 1/2 cup canned pumpkin
- 2 tbsp cocoa powder
- 1 tsp pumpkin pie spice
- 1/2 tsp vanilla extract
- 1 tbsp sugar

What to do:
1. Place the milk, pumpkin, cocoa powder, pumpkin pie spice, and vanilla extract in a blender and blend until smooth and frothy.
2. Pour the mixture into a saucepan over medium heat and add the sugar.
3. Stir until the mixture is steaming but not boiling.
4. Pour into two mugs and serve.

pumpkin spice coffee creamer

Servings: 20+

What you need:

- 14 oz can of sweetened condensed milk
- 2 cups milk
- 3 tbsp canned pumpkin
- 3 tbsp maple syrup
- 1 tbsp vanilla
- 1 tsp pumpkin pie spice

What to do:

1. Pour the sweetened condensed milk and the milk into a quart sized jar.
2. Add in the pumpkin, maple syrup, vanilla, and pumpkin pie spice.
3. Put the lids on the jar and shake the jar vigorously.
4. Store in the refrigerator for up to 2 weeks.

Banana Pumpkin Smoothie

Servings: 1

What you need:
- 1/2 cup canned pumpkin
- 1/2 banana
- 1/2 cup milk
- 1/2 tsp pumpkin pie spice
- 1/2 tsp brown sugar
- 1/4 tsp cinnamon
- 1/4 tsp vanilla extract
- 1/2 cup crushed ice

What to do:
1. Place all of the ingredients in your blender.
2. Blend for 1 minute or until smooth.
3. Pour into a glass and serve immediately.

Pumpkin Pie Smoothie

Servings: 1

What you need:
- 1/2 cup canned pumpkin
- 1/2 large banana, peeled
- 1/2 cup coconut milk
- 1/2 tbsp honey
- 1/4 tsp vanilla extract
- 1 tsp pumpkin pie spice
- 2 ice cubes

What to do:
1. Combine all of the ingredients in a blender and blend until smooth.
2. Pour into a glass and serve.

Pumpkin Protein Smoothie

Servings: 1

What you need:
- 1 cup Greek yogurt
- 1/2 cup canned pumpkin
- 1 tbsp honey
- 1 tsp pumpkin pie spice
- 2 tbsp whey protein powder

What to do:
1. Place all of the ingredients in a blender and blend until smooth.
2. Pour into a glass and serve.

Oatmeal Pumpkin Smoothie

Servings: 1

What you need:
- 1/4 cup canned pumpkin
- 1/4 cup rolled oats
- 1/2 tsp pumpkin spice seasoning
- 1 tsp maple syrup
- 1/2 tsp brown sugar
- 1/2 cup plain Greek yogurt
- 3/4 cup coconut milk

What to do:
1. Place all of the ingredients in a blender and blend until smooth.
2. Pour into a glass and serve.

Pumpkin Pie Milkshake

Servings: 3

What you need:
- 1 cup milk
- 1/2 cup plain Greek yogurt
- 1/2 cup canned pumpkin
- 1 banana; peeled, cut up, and frozen
- 1 tbsp honey
- 1 tsp pumpkin pie spice
- 1/2 tsp cinnamon
- 1/2 tsp vanilla extract
- 1/2 ice cubes

What to do:
1. Place all ingredients in a blender and blend until smooth.
2. Pour into glasses and serve.

Pumpkin Cider Beer

Servings: 4

What you need:
- 3 bottles of Blue Moon Pumpkin Ale
- 1/2 bottle sparkling cider
- 4 cinnamon sticks
- 4 lemon wedges
- Cinnamon

What to do:
1. Get 4 glasses or jars.
2. Put a cinnamon stick in each glass.
3. Fill each glass 3/4 full of Blue Moon.
4. Fill each glass the rest of the way with the sparkling cider.
5. Squeeze a little lemon juice in each glass.
6. Place a lemon wedge on each glass rim.
7. Top each drink with a sprinkle of cinnamon.

Pumpkin Pie White Hot Chocolate

Servings: 2

What you need:
- 2 cups milk
- 1/2 cup white chocolate chips
- 2 tbsp canned pumpkin
- 1 tbsp corn starch
- 1 tbsp vanilla extract
- 1 shot of rum
- Marshmallows

What to do:
1. In a medium saucepan over low heat, add the milk, chocolate chips, pumpkin, corn starch, and vanilla extract.
2. Whisk together until combined and let simmer for 5-7 minutes or until chocolate is melted and liquid is thickened.
3. Pour into two coffee mugs and stir in the rum.
4. Top with marshmallows before serving.

PumPkin ButtereD Rum

Servings: 6

What you need:

- 1/4 cup unsalted butter, softened
- 3/4 cup brown sugar
- 1/3 cup pumpkin butter
- 1 tsp pumpkin pie spice
- A pinch of salt
- Dark rum
- Hot water
- Whipped cream

What to do:

1. In a mixing bowl, cream together the butter, brown sugar, pumpkin butter, pumpkin pie spice, and salt.
2. Add 2 tbsp of butter mixture to the bottom of each glass or mug.
3. Add 2 oz of rum to each glass.
4. Fill each glass with boiling water and stir to mix well.
5. Top with whipped cream.

Pumpkin White Russian

Servings: 1

What you need:

- 4 oz pumpkin spice Kahlua
- 2 oz vodka
- 3 oz heavy cream

What to do:

1. Fill a glass with ice.
2. Pour in the Kahlua, vodka, and heavy cream and stir.
3. Serve immediately.

Butterscotch Pumpkin Drink

Servings: 1

What you need:
- 3 oz Kahlua Pumpkin Spice
- 3 oz butterscotch schnapps
- 2 oz heavy cream

What to do:
1. Place all of the ingredients in a shaker with ice.
2. Shake well to mix.
3. Pour in a martini glass and serve.

Pumpkin Cheesecake Cocktail

Servings: 1

What you need:
- 1/3 cup milk
- 3 tbsp pumpkin spice liqueur
- 1 tbsp cinnamon schnapps
- 1 tsp instant cheesecake pudding mix
- Caramel
- Graham cracker crumbs
- Whipped cream
- Pumpkin Spice

What to do:
1. Mix the milk, pumpkin spice liqueur, cinnamon schnapps, and pudding mix in a shaker with ice for 30 seconds.
2. Dip the rim of a martini glass in caramel, then graham cracker crumbs.
3. Strain the drink into the martini glass.
4. Top with whipped cream and a dash of pumpkin spice.

pumpkin Martini

Servings: 1

What you need:
- 2 oz vanilla vodka
- 1 oz Kahlua
- 3 tbsp canned pumpkin
- 1/2 cup milk
- 2 tsp honey
- Crushed graham crackers
- Ice
- A pinch of pumpkin pie spice
- Cinnamon stick

What to do:
1. Rim a martini glass with honey and dip the rim into crushed graham crackers. Set aside.
2. Place the pumpkin and milk in a cocktail shaker and shake well.
3. Add the vodka, Kahlua, and ice to the shaker and shake well.
4. Strain into the prepared martini glass.
5. Top with pumpkin pie spice and garnish with a cinnamon stick.

About the Author

Hannie P. Scott, Full-Time Mom and Food Blogger

Driven by her desire for cooking for others (and herself), Hannie spends a lot of time in the kitchen! She enjoys sharing her love of food with the world by creating "no-nonsense" recipe books that anyone can use to make delicious meals.

Hannie attended the University of Southern Mississippi and received a Bachelor's degree in Nutrition & Dietetics. She enjoys cooking and experimenting with food. She hopes to inspire readers and help them build confidence in their cooking. All Hannie's recipes are easy-to-prepare with easy-to-acquire ingredients.

For more recipes, cooking tips, and Hannie's blog, visit:

www.Hanniepscott.com

Notes

Notes

Notes

Notes

Notes

Notes

Made in the USA
Columbia, SC
08 October 2024